MYSTICAL SHE

MYSTIC LOVE

Made with ❤ on the Notion Press Platform
www.notionpress.com

<u>To god</u>,

Without whom this book would never came into existence.

My imagination is the best thing God has given to me...

<u>To my family</u>,

Who didn't know even that

If a book like this exists or not

but still they never nagged in any new skill I want to learn.

Always supported me in every progressive task I do.

Thank you everyone

<u>To my friend family</u>,

They know every incident that the coming content is based on,

and I believe them they will never misuse my trust...

Thanks everyone

-Shivang

Contents

Contents

Contents

Foreword

When I first had the privilege of reading the poems composed in this book, I was struck by the raw honesty and profound intimacy that reverberates from each verse.

Shivang's words have a truly remarkable ability to cut through the noise of everyday life and speak directly to the heart, evoking a range of emotions.

These poems have the power to transport the reader, allowing us to see the world through the poet's eyes and feel the weight of his joys, sorrows, and everything in between.

Each poem is a window into the poet's soul, inviting us to empathize, to reflect, and to appreciate the beauty that can be found in the most fleeting and fragile of human experiences.

I encourage you to approach these poems with an open heart and mind. Allow yourself to be moved and inspired by the depth of emotion and virtuosity.

In these poems, you will perhaps find a profound exploration of love in all its complexities - the elation, the heartbreak, the longing, the hope.

It is my sincere hope that you will discover within these poems a kindred spirit, a reflection of your own experiences, and a newfound appreciation for the power of language to illuminate human emotions.

-Kabir Agarwal

Contact Kabir:

FOREWORD

“**Instagram:** *sense_science*”

E-Mali: Sciencekabir@gmail.com

Preface

<u>hey friends!</u>

In this collection of romantic verses, the author invites you to embark on a journey through the intricacies of love.

Each poem in this book is a melody of emotions, crafted with tenderness and sincerity.

From the whispers of longing to the crescendo of passion, these words dance on the pages, painting vivid portraits of love's many shades.

Through heartfelt verses, the suthor explores the depths of the heart, celebrating the beauty of connection and the power of affection.

Join him in this lyrical exploration of love, where every stanza is a testament to the magic that resides in the human heart.

Prologue

lets begin with the context of the book.

all the poems are written in an imaginary manner that if i would have also been through similar circumstances then what would i will have been doing to just living the thrust of emotions blissfully.

through these poems, you will experience different stages of attachment (other than family) and the upcoming detachment.

this book will lightly tell you the senses of love, so read it slowly and peacefully....

-Mystic Love

1. ME BEING CRUSHED !

…

I wanted to go

wit da flow

but went against her

in da flow of

Billions

…

-Mystic Love

Theme of the phrase…

These lines are of the glamorous times

when I was taken…

taken by the goddess herself ! but,

I went in debt of feelings

And got undeserving...

Here, in this time,

I let my feelings unfurl and

It struck her damn hard that

Thereafter we barely talk

emergence of this thought

You know sometimes you get too much into feeling that you lost your mind and if you are a person like me who loves to play with their own emotions then, hey! Listen this, you are at the right book,

The idea of the phrase is so simple but no one will understand it without this explanation.

Her name symbolizes river, water, stream etc. so I just symbolized her with 'the flow' and wrote the above phrase, now read it again!

2. WE ARE OURS !

-the right perspective

I never loved you selfishly
so never shall I say
"YOU ARE MINE"
I never loved you selflessly
always held and respected my feelings
that emerge for you Helplessly
so never shall I say
"I AM YOUR'S"
I believe 'we are one'
I embraced our 'Romantic Fun'
for me, you are sun;
for you, I might be none
so ever shall I say,
"WE ARE OURS"

-Mystic Love

Theme of the lyrics

the given shot is simple and 'to the point'.

See,

You should never love someone selfishly

because they are also humans

and you can't force your feelings on them.

You should never love someone selflessly

because if you do so, then you are just

disrespecting your feelings for them

and that's not good.

you all love someone (after family) that

they mean everything to us sometimes

so, with respect to that feeling

you both are one and that's why

you must say

“We are ours”

the build of this idea !

I just wanted the world to understand that love is not selfless and selfish.

Love is the stream which flows from two different points but merge at the point in life where god let them do so.

so, love is always ours,

not mine,

not yours,

it's totally ours…

3. A Glimpse of My Attitude

I ma' little too much shy
Cannot contact straight in the eye
But still don't know why?
I am lost in the thoughts of
YOU AND I …
Waitin' for our boats to tie
Till the future day, I die
I m' not gonna lie
Just hate seeing best friends sayin good bye
But the point is:
I m still lost in the thoughts of
YOU AND I …

-Mystic Love

theme of my attitude

no need of any theme !...

4. The School Age (#boys)

I've got a decent face
With a pretty decent nose
People don't like to embrace
Yup! That's my case.
Teeth aren't a red flag
They are white as pearl
Skin is fair too, but not fair enough
To attract a pretty girl.
Acne isn't the problem
I believe in inner beauty
Still I tried every skin product
to impress the second row's cutie.
confidence is the USP
which I carry in detail
but at the precious moment it dies
and I fail.
eyes got the main roll
they are there to read gestures
of the girl, ya, that's the last toll
but at the moment they loss control.
I am not afraid to die alone
My fear is to the fact that if I never try
In the era which is heart break prone

I surely will sit depressed alone.

-Mystic Love

theme

...

The more you suffer

The more you understand.

...

From Where?

I m a boy, at the age of acne, the age of insecurities, yes, the age of suffer, but it's all imaginary,

The further you grow in life the farther you got to go from these lies.

I think it in a different perspective,

At this particular time of life,

We have uncertain brains, and even we don't have enough experience that we can make good decisions out of our life.

So, god don't want us to get attracted by outer beauty instead he teaches us to look for the reality…

PHASE 1- THE ATTRACTION

This is a section of book which contains poems in series of all imaginations I had in the attraction phase

5. I-spy

I sat aside
Thinking of my crush
I don't know why
But I wanna rush

Sittin' around with tears in the eye
Waitin' for someone to come and say
I-spy !
Stuck in the thought:
Whether should I live or die
I just wanted to say this universe a good bye !
-Mystic Love

reasons for its existance

This was the first time I had the feeling of what it feels like when you had a crush on someone…

…

I was unable to control anything

…

6. The Gist of You !

The gist of you

Imprinted on my mind with a great view

Just give that one little clue

To possessify the gist of you

You love me?

Hope you do

Never mind

I love you too

Girl, you got me crazy

Now just let me slide through

To the view

Yea that's new

Yea those eyes that count in two

Yes, those eyes that dye in blue

Yea my crazy mind you knew

All this love in me it grew

For you

Yea that's true

I'm the first in the que

You, I pursue

Your looks, I withdrew

Your hooks, I drew

Your books, I review

Your talks, I undue
Yea…
It's the gist of you.

-Mystyic Love

How I got this done?

I was not in mood to write something but still I want to…

So, I just grab my pen and start writing in rhyme

n……

got that piece…

7. Lone Pain

I heard the sky cry...

I saw the pain
In her rain
the drops were salty
Not sugarcane
They were tears in vain
The glance of "Lone Pain" …

-Mystic Love

when I wrote this ?

It was feb 20 when it was raining hard and I couldn't stop myself from writing down the pain of the sky

That's why it goes like:

...

I heard the sky cry

...

8. our LOVE CASE

One-two three countin' days
Observing my love.
Just finding psycho tricks
To live in better ways
Yup! That's our love case.
You showed up to me like nothing happened
Oh! I forget, you are unaware of the fact
Of the war in my heart
Which I never lickened
No-nope, it's not at all your fault.
It's just about our love case.
I know, like me for yours',
You also fear about my heart
And I understand, for love, it's an important part
Isn't just a game of dart,
That's our "Love Art"
I promise,
All your flaws are mine to embrace
Yup! That's Me with You type case
All my stress and fear is cured
By one pretty smile on your face
Yes…
That's our love case

Still you are free
It's not a pressure from my edge
'for you to be with me' I pledge
Still-
You will be my only love case
And I may inscribe you in my life
with the pronoun "SHE"
that will be the example of true love-
"OUR LOVE CASE"

-Mystic Love

theme

I wrote these lyrics as a message to her that this is not a pressure from my edge,

I just want to convey these feelings to you in order to let you know that you are sent from heaven above.

9. World as Heaven

This world would be a
heavenly place to be
if I could dance to your rhythm
in your presence with glee...

-Mystic Love

theme

I was lost in the world of yours

I now just wanted to get on your rhythm and dance with your presence among the people who thought love to be secondary…

10. if I Could !

If I could look at you
Without my hearth in me,
I would have given it to you
The day I tasted your beauty
With my eyes !

-Mystic Love

theme

In my imagination, I loved her so much that if I could still observe her without my heart in me, then I would not hesitate to give it to her…

PHASE 1

THE END

PHASE 2- THE DEPRESSION

The moments when in my imagination I lost her

11. The Loss

The love of mine is flown
I am searching in the ocean to see
If she had drowned
Looking for her in the sky
And the land which is heart break prone…

-Mystic Love

theme

in my imagination, my being with her ended, and I was lost at this point in life that where should I look for her…

…

land which is heart break prone

…

12. My Vast Expectations

I wanted to hug the sky
But then I realized her vast expectations
Which would never settle in my arms
So, I said a hurtful
Bye!!

-Mystic Love

theme

In the given extract of my imagination I was longing for something beyond my reach.

I am not at the level at which I would fulfil her desires so

...

My arms became short enough to let her go

...

MY realization

I wrote this when I realized that the person I was in love with (in my imagination) had expectations from me that I won't be able to fulfill in my whole life that's the reason I wrote the above freestyle...

13. Realization

I tried to touch
Her innocence
But then I realized that
All roses have thorns…

-Mystic Love

theme

The given piece of my imagination explores the facts that you have to overcome to love the one with full devotion.

There are flaws which you might not like but you love them truly if you have the courage to ignore them.

The truest example is the unconditional love of your parents towards you

...

All roses have thorns

Dare to embrace them

...

14. False Confession

I tried to confess
My feelings for her
Surprisingly!
That's the time I realized
"for me, her feelings never were."

-Mystic Love

THE CONDITION

This is what I heard when I confessed and tried my best to
embrace her

The phase of my life (in imagination) which is the most addicting
when you realize she doesn't even care who you are…

…

For me her feelings never were

…

ひつ

15. THE air

The day was fair
I was in a bus
Not emptyhanded
I was holding a teddy bear
I rolled down my window
To feel the air
Of the love and care
Which was never there

-Mystic Love

theme

I wrote this to depict the feeling when you are with many people but still feel insecure of the fact that you have no one like you around…

the understanding

Even at the worst of your life, there is someone that will still be there by your side and that is your family.

Hey, focus here,

Even if you don't have family then you will always have the one who created your family, who created you,

THE GOD, you can find his significance around you in the form of nature (grass, air, sky, plants, ground, dark, light etc:)

16. SKY full of STARS

I remembered the night
With all crowded bars
We were on top of our senses
At the top of our powers

We avoided the smoking people
Avoided burning cigars
We don't need toxins
We loved playing guitars

I lost faith in the nature,
when she took away you
And left me with scars
I was left with the love letters
I stored in jars

I was sad because of the fate we dreamed of
Could never be our's
I started spending my lone nights
On the top of city towers
Watching you gone between sparkling stars

You are my sky full of stars
I gave you my heart…

-Mystic Love

theme

...

She was gone,

Not from my senses,

But from this hatred filled world

...

Here, I used the phrase "smoking people" which symbolizes the people who creates confusion between us and misguide us.

the IDEA !

You know imagination is a nation with limitless boundaries, the more you travel in it the more you explore.

So just to explore the sad phase of me, I imagined as if my love was gone between the stars and now I am drowning in the nostalgia of the moments we spent together in the top of our spirits.

PHASE 2

THE END

PHASE 3- THE OVERCOME

Thoughts of me when I want to be the one again

17. My expectations

Sat aside I once thought, what if I was sad
And if it was easier to live like a bot…

> Once sitting in the midnight
> In the pale moon
> I wondered if, I had a boon
> Thought of my life
> Which I will transform soon
> Yet still sitting in the midnight
> In the pale moon
> Through the noon gliding in thoughts
> Of soon becoming, My parents moon

The dark clouds of despair

Soon started to gather

It was a bright sunny day

But soon changed to a stormy weather

Hoped 'someone was by my side'

And we've walked this lonely road

Together

> Suddenly out of the greyish weather
> The light appeared
> I questioned myself that whether

Should I thrive, or being stuck here is better
Or should I call my first step, which might seem bitter,
But my aim is to become the version of myself
That is softly engineered to get her
Here 'her' symbolizes the beauty of the one
That if I was pointed by her with a gun
I wouldn't run
Instead I would regret my steps,
And fly them as fun
Just sitting depressed to the thing
"what I have done"

So, to not get in this type of situation
I will put in my thoughts the best punctuation
I would try my best to become the world's salvation
And I wrote this poem to
Get me and my thoughts in the best relation.
-Mystic Love

theme

This is one of my earliest poems which are straight in meaning so they don't need specific theme.

18. ONE DAY !

Living in bed
Almost dead
I once thought

One day
I thought to start living
Oh! Alas! I forgot, I've left the beginning
There is a way
Start from now
To the mighty's principles
I bow

One day
Hanging around with thoughts of dust
A sudden thought came of being first
It seems a bit hard to fly from this depth
With a gust
But it's not the end I trust
Believe in god's choices I must
Grease myself with positivity, never rust
Should not load with much
Because I am a balloon which bursts

-Mystic Love

At the time of application

I wrote this in sense of motivation but I don't know why I ended it
in wrong sense.

Why I should burst?

PHASE 3

THE END

PHASE 4- THE BESTIE

Time came by and pass by but the truth I got to know in every phase is that, your bestie is the one with whom you can share things which even sometimes your parents might not understand and she will always support you for the best of you

19. you gotta believe

If I told you in your face
You are the one for me to embrace, you won't believe...
If I told you, you earned my trust
Yes, you are totally worthy
And this feeling must never rust
You won't believe...
I want to make you realize
You mean a lot to me
You are the one, I recognize
You won't believe...
I want you to think
About the reality of us, which we will link
Yes, these words quoted in ink
The contact of us, never blink
The thoughts of, in a sync
The bond of us, never shrink
The love of us, interlink
Yup, this is our friendship
You gotta believe...

-Mystic Love

theme

In the current world,

Most people don't know their value

And are living feelinglessly like robot

And to those, this is my polite message that there is a person

Who loves you unconditionally…

…

You gotta believe

…

the fact

We, people are so overconfident being so underconfident that we even doubt our appreciation.

So being a helper of yours I want to clarify that stop being underconfident and work on your image and self...

20. The Bestie Humor

In today's world

Pencils became pointless
Pens became inkless
Love became bondless
Life became meaningless

Today, in the world of mean
You are the one on my main screen
In my life acting as a disprine
And making my thoughts, my life
Clean…

-Mystic Love

theme

You know that after family there is a person who will always help
you to get the right track in your life

That's the reality…

And for those

I wrote this humorous phrase just to make a humorous bond
between us…

…

Some are disprine to your life

…

PHASE 4

THE END

21. A MESSAGE TO YOU

truth to the one

Mystic love says you hie !

Welcome to my work, my apple pie

You don't know mw for sure

But let me tell you,

All prejudices on me are a lie

For you, I might be a bad guy

But I bet for sure,

You don't have the reason why?

Because I am not that simple

I hid my feelings deep within me

Just to see the real people faking lies

Mother told me I have to be clever

To live in this world, but I insisted

I'll never,

Truth will behold the power forever

I endeavor

People judge you in their eye

You sometimes feel it's a war cry

But you aren't a soldier until…

You insist your courage to never die
I understand you will be having a garden
With a cutie and two butterflies
But you will have to believe the truth of the warden
Of the world which fakes you lies

-Mystic Love

the hidden message

In the first two stanzas I am letting you understand that people are judged just on the basis of the prejudices already made on them by others and this too when they don't even have the reason to be judged by others.

Moving on to the next stanza I let you know that how some parents tell you that being true and simple is not good for yourself but I interrupt that its not true. Truth will hold the power forever…

Afterwards,

I continue by telling you that still people will judge you but you are a soldier if you never let your courage die

The most beautiful stanza at the last which depicts the future that at some point of time you will have your home with your wife and two cute kids and still you are not free, you will have to understand the truth of the nature(warden) which fakes you lies…

Thank You !

Hope you liked the poems and please also wait for my upcoming books

And I will cover topics like:

self-development, romantic plays and much more.

love you readers....

Bye

Meet you soon!

-Mystic Love

-Shivang

About The Author

Shivang, another teenager who experienced the romantic perspective of life but he just didn't think of it, but brought his thoughts to reality by breaking cage of overthinking and putting his thoughts on paper in simple rhyming language so that others can get what he experienced in his teenage…

He motivates teens to not just stop at the stage of dreaming but move on to the next stage of carving dreams to reality.

In his school, he is famous for his self-written motivational speeches, poetry and many more vocal performances because he never let google guide him because he believed that god gave him a powerful machine called brain which gets him idea directly from the one above!

His dreaming style never gets old, he even makes the oldest person in this world to rethink about what life really is.

He also emphasizes on the truth that if someone other can create a blueprint of you life then is your life worth living?

For example:

Here is a blue print of most of you people's life:

- Birth
- Go to school
- Get a degree
- Get a job
- Marriage

- Make love
- Have kids
- Work till your kids became independent
- Retirement
- Think of what I could have become if I did something better
- Die

Is this your life?

If not then work independently and rule your own kingdom

Thank you for reading this book…

-Shivang

Contact the author:

Insta: me.shivang

e-mail: mystic.lover.16@gmail.com

The End ...

The Writer:

-MYSTIC LOVE
-SHIVANG BHATI